Sid's helpful handwriting hints

Follow Genius's Helpful Hints and *you* can have handwriting as brill as mine.

Handwriting is a skill, like riding a bike, or swimming. You can only get good at a skill if you practise it. You learn by **doing** it, the more you **practise** the **better** you get.

My handwriting takes me absolutely ages and still looks awful.

Practice makes perfect!

My name is Tatty Tricia xxx

Some things you need to learn before you rush off to practise your handwriting.

1. Make sure that you have something good to write with.

2. Make sure that you are **sitting** comfortably at a desk or table. (Not lying down.)

3. Make sure that you are holding your pen or pencil in a proper way.

4. Your paper should be in a good position to write on.

5. Turn off the telly!

1. Sounds silly, but no-one can write properly with a blunt stubby pencil or worn out biro. Try writing with a lot of different pens and pencils.

2. No-one can write very well if they are swinging upside down from the light shades.

3. Try writing using the wrong end or holding it at the end farthest away from the paper.

4. Not too close, not too far away, and if you are left handed at a slight angle.

5. Aw, Sid you are a bore!

THE RIGHT WAY TO SIT

1. Feet on ground.
2. Head up.
3. Chest away from the table, about a hand's width away.

THE RIGHT WAY TO HOLD THE PEN

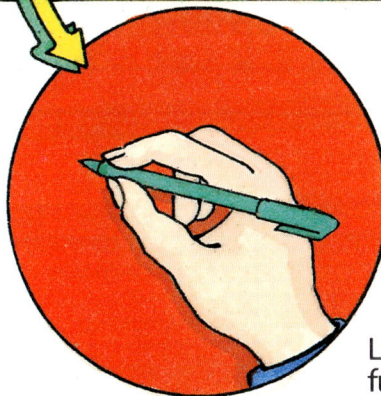

1. Hold between thumb and index finger, resting on second finger.
2. Don't hold too tight.
3. Hand rests lightly on table.

Left handed? Hold a little further away from the point.

HOW TO POSITION THE PAPER

Right handed
1. Just on the right hand side of your body.
2. Turned a little bit to the left.
3. Away, but not too far, from the edge of the table.

Left handed
1. Just on the left hand side of your body.
2. Turned a little bit to the right.
3. Away, but not too far, from the edge of the table.

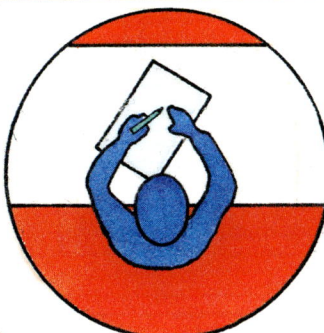

When I write for a long time my hand and fingers begin to hurt.

That probably means you're holding the pen too tightly *or* you're pressing too hard.

Every time you start to write, check:
1. How you're sitting.
2. How you're holding the pen.
3. Paper position.

3

Joined up writing

Some kids call joined up writing 'grown up writing'. Being able to do it is part of being grown up.

Is this like the handwriting you do? Or is yours different?

It takes quite a lot of practice at first, but it's quicker, looks better and is more fun than other writing.

First, practise joining up the letters with each other, ab, ac, ad and so on until you reach zz. Try the first few here. Continue on your own using lined paper.

Remember: you don't have to join every single letter.

This is the joined up handwriting we do at Splott Street School. We can all do it very quickly except for Weedy. He's much too lazy.

Z Z Z z z z z z z

abacada
bcbdbeb
cdcecfc
dedfdgd

Joining up letters is like making patterns. Mixing them up can make super patterns. Try copying these first, using lined paper. Can you invent some of your own?

nnnnnnnnnnnnnnnnnnnn

amamamamamamamamamam

VVVVVVVVVVVVVVVVVVVVVV

wowowowowowowowowow

cocococococococococococococococococo

mimimimimimimimimimimimimimimimi

Adding to your patterns can be even more fun. What other shapes can you invent? Draw the first few here and then continue on your own.

Did you notice that most of these were letters?

5

The most important joined up word for everyone is their signature, or the way they sign their name.

Here are some famous signatures.

Sid

Keng Tak

Claudia

Gus.

Tricia

Gargoyle

Skulk

Hatchet

Reshma

This is Ronald the cat.

Here are some famous people.

MAUD

ELSIE

WEEDY

ROGER THE ROTTER

What do you think their signatures would be like?
Try writing them here.

Look at the signatures carefully. Now practise your own signature.

WWWWWhhhhg sssooooo rrrruuummmmbangbangb

What a good idea – stretching out words to make sounds.

Can you think of some long stretchy words for these? Practise them first, then write them here in your own best handwriting!

Bees after Weedy's honey sandwich.

A train going very fast.

An owl calling at night.

A crocodile having its breakfast.

Tops of the letters h, d and b are the right height.

The writing is a nice size.

Tails of the letters g, p and y are the right length.

Here's my own perfect handwriting! Remember: lots of practice of patterns and writing makes perfect.

The spacing between the words is just right.

7

Design a border

Letter patterns can make ghoulishly good border designs. Here's one I did for Skulk's new menu.

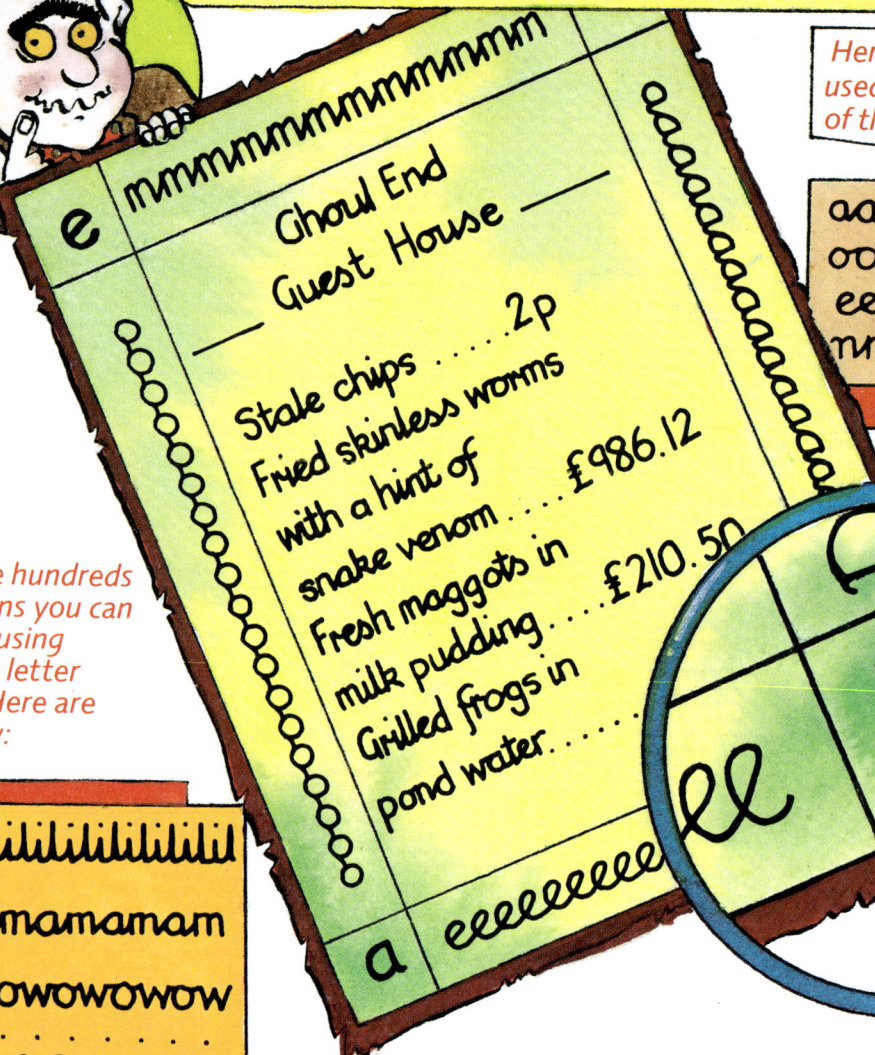

Here are the letter patterns Gargoyle used to make the border. Practise lots of them to make up your own border.

mmmmmmmmmmmmm

e

oooooooooooo

aaaaaaaaaaaaa

Ghoul End Guest House

Stale chips 2p
Fried skinless worms
with a hint of
snake venom £986.12
Fresh maggots in
milk pudding £210.50
Grilled frogs in
pond water......

a eeeeeeeee

aaaaaaaaaaaaaaaaaaa
ooooooooooooooooooo
eeeeeeeeeeeeeeeeeee
mmmmmmmmmmmmm

There are hundreds of patterns you can make by using joined up letter shapes. Here are just a few:

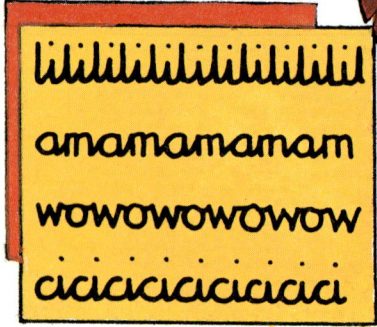

lililililililililil

amamamamam

wowowowowow

cicicicicicicici

Invent some of your own. It's easy when you try.

Finish off the border on this menu. Then fill in the rest of the menu in your best joined up writing. Make up your own name for a restaurant or hotel and then some disgusting things to eat with silly prices.

Drawing flowing patterns can help your handwriting a lot.

Good handwriting is really making patterns that people can understand.

menu

EATS   PRICE

Looking at handwriting

Here's some handwriting done by the Splott Street School kids. One is good, some are not too bad, but some are pretty awful. Can you sort them out?

Mark

I am NoT a BuLLY and I will bAsh up anybody WHo says that I am.

Roger

My father was in the pig shed. You could tell which one was father because he had his old hat on.

Lisa

Can a cross eyed teacher control her pupils?

Weedy

The day stoob on the durning beck eating his dread anb dutter, it got so hot, the silly

ermayen whichja enyuh eustunshy. Bunt liv in tend mew bun wti Uni in. Bunb ten bineyyen enjrunter.

Emma

Reshma

Schooldinners areso bad at SplottStreetwe are going onstrike for shorterlunchtimes.

Our teacher taught us how to preserve flowers by pressing them but when I tried it with a tadpole it went rotten!

Claudia

Put a sample of your handwriting here.

Collect other people's handwriting to look at too.

Is it easy to read?

Trust Sid to ask the most important question.

Are the tails of the letters like g, p, y long enough?

Are the spaces between the words right?

Are the tops of the letters like h, d, b high enough?

What to look for *Look at each of the Splott Street kids' handwriting on the opposite page and then answer these questions. We tell you what we think on page 22.*

Put a ✓ *for Yes; a* ✗ *for No.*

The writing which gets the most ✓ is the best. (How did yours do?) We've done the first one for you. (If you need any more help, look at the good handwriting examples on pages 4 and 7.)

	Reshma	Weedy	Claudia	Mark	Emma	Roger	Lisa	You
Is it easy to read?	✗							
Are the letters on the line?	✓							
Are the capital letters in the right place?	✓							
Are all the letters the right way round?	✓							
Are the letter tops high enough?	✓							
Are the letter tails long enough?	✓							
Are the spaces between the words right?	✗							

How to be an ace forger!

This book tells me the rules for an ace forger. Good copying really pays off!

FORGERY FOR PLEASURE AND GAIN

BANK OF ENGLAND

£7

I promise to pay the bearer on demand the sum of

SEVEN POUNDS

DOPE 6 4287
London for the Gov'r and Comp'n of the Bank of England.

EUR
D. H. F Sumptuous
CHIEF CASHIER.
DOPE 6 4287

£7

Forge this £7 note carefully here.

BANK OF ENGLAND

£7

SEVEN POUNDS

£7

1. Copy very carefully.

2. Speed is less important than getting it right.

3. Practise each part before you do the final copy.

This is the last Will and Testament
Dated 26th September 1989

Of me, Gargoyle, being of unsound body and mind, I leave all my worldly baddies to my disgusting friend Hatchet. He can have my collection of dead and revolting beetles and spiders. He must also promise to write in the Ghoul End News what a stinker I was to everyone everywhere. Signed .... *Gargoyle.*
Witness .... *His mum*

If you follow the rules for forgers, like Hatchet did here, **you** can get everything Gargoyle is leaving to Hatchet.

Forge another copy of Gargoyle's Will here.

Don't forget to write your own name instead of Hatchet's!

Remember: accurate copying pays off.

Don't be a Space Invader

Cor, isn't Sara's writing difficult to read? It's because she doesn't leave any space between the words.

That's why we call her the Space Invader!

But didn't I sign it nicely?

A SPACE STORY

Infourteenhundredandninetyonethe
braveSeaCaptainChristinaCucumber
setouttosailacrosstheAtlanticOcean
toprovethattheworldwasround.She
sailedonandonuntiloneday sheand
hershipfelloffttheedgeoftheworld.She
haddiscoveredthattheworldwasround
afterallandshehadalsobecomethe
first Captainofaspaceship .

Sara

She hasn't left any space at the sides either. You should always have a good margin all round.

Go through Sara's story carefully and put a red line where a space should be. The first three are done for you.

Write Sara's story here in your best joined up writing. Don't forget to put in the spaces between the words.

You could put a decorative border in this space. Try using the letter C, like this.

cccccccccccc
cccccccccccc
ccccccccccccccc

Colouring it could make it look even better.

REMEMBER
Words are like people. They need a little space.

A SPACE STORY

Check your spaces on page 22.

Moneypincher writes like some kid who sticks capital letters all over the place.

What Bong doesn't know is that Miss Moneypincher has put the capital letters in the wrong place **on purpose**. If Bong writes out the misplaced capital letters he will discover a secret message from Moneypincher. (You will too.)

SINISTER SPY

Here's how to do it.

Put a red circle round every capital letter that is in the wrong place. Then write out the letters you have circled to reveal the secret message.

Write Miss Moneypincher's secret message here.

SECRET SERVICE

so secret
we don't have
an address

no-one must
know the date

DarlinG JamEs,

Beware, THe trAiTors CaugHt onE of our TeAm aND Grilled him Until hiS Brains bEgan to Fry and his nOstRils bEgan to sTeam. THE poor guY held out until he turned GreEn enough To Make a frEsh lettuce look pink but then he hAd to spill the beAns. The beAns were eAten by GarGoyle quicker tHan a liTtle BrOwn Owl cOuld Light A fire by rubbing two cubs TogethEr.

So take care my love they have the code.

Miss Moneypincher

Why not send secret messages to your friends using Moneypincher's code?

When to use capital letters

1. To begin a sentence. That's usually after a full stop.

2. The first letter of a name.

3. To draw attention, for example — in a title.

ALWAYS keep an eye open for misplaced capital letters.

The answer is on page 22.

Shape up your writing

I found this poem about a strange cat and I've written it inside the shape of a cat. I'm really tired now...

Start here

Writing inside the outline shape of whatever it is you are writing about can be great fun and add a lot of interest for anyone reading your writing.

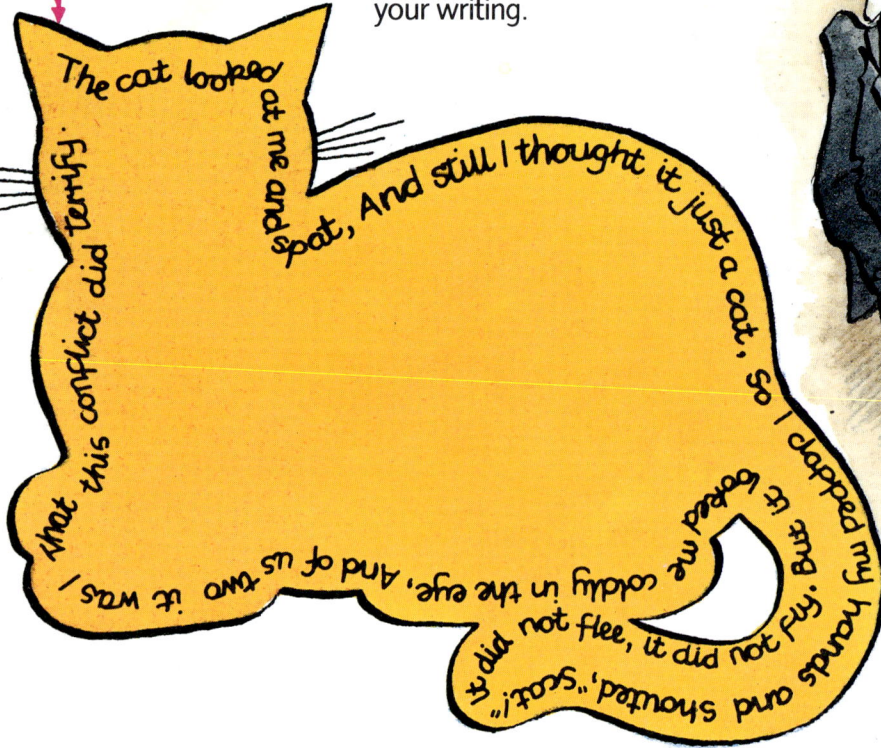

The cat looked at me and spat, And still I thought it just a cat, So I clapped my hands and shouted, "Scat!" It did not flee, it did not fly. But it looked me coolly in the eye, And of us two it was I, what this conflict did terrify.

Baaah, who wants to write or read about silly cats. I've written a much nicer poem about lovely sewers.

Underneath the drain cover,
There's a world of murk and slime,
Of rats and snakes in dinersewers,
Where loos flush all the time.

Which poem do you like the best?

Can you copy Skulk's poem? Write in a spiral inside the drain cover. We've started it for you.

Find some writing or, better still, make up your own. Write inside the car and dinosaur shapes. You can use some of these words.

fast   race   vroom   whoosh   screech   big

gigantic   lumbering   little brain   extinct

Underneath the drain cover

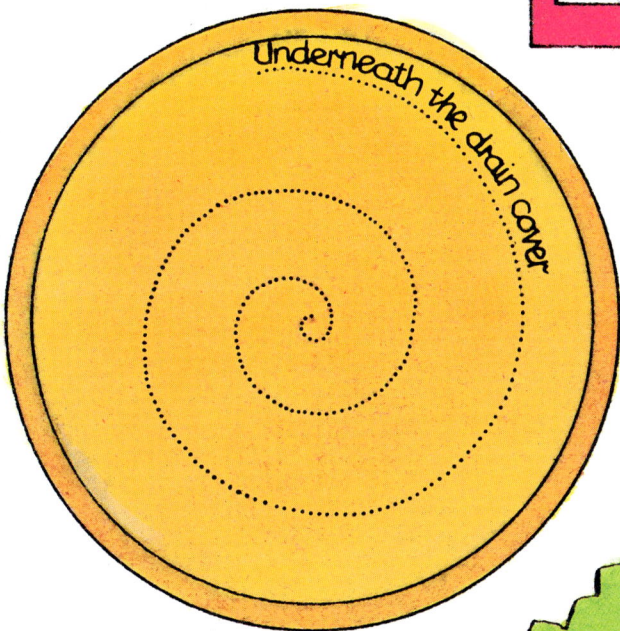

Why not draw lots of shapes for yourself and then write inside them?

Always make sure that your writing fits into the space you have available.

19

Writing you can read

Remember! When you are writing something that someone else will read it must be easy to read.

The headstones in a graveyard have to be legible (easy to read). Can you finish off the ones that Roger's started? Can you make up some more of your own?

ROGER'S GRAVEYARD FOR DEAD PETS AND INSECTS

Geniuses like me use the word *legible*.

CYRIL SLUG

Here lies FRED FROG

R.I.P. SAM SNAIL Tho' slo quick to go 2ND JUNE 1988

Here lies BILLY BEE buzzed off 1 ST OCT 1989

R.I.P.

All that's left of BRENDA BLUEBOTTLE

MAY SHE REST IN PEACE

MOLLY MOUSE Went down her last hole on 3rd JULY 1986

Graffiti wall

Here's your chance to write silly messages and things for other people to read. Don't forget to write in your best joined up handwriting!

Gargoyle Loves....

Why not do some in different colours or brighten them with a highlighter?

THE LOCH NESS MONSTER IS SEVEN MILES WIDE AND NEARLY TWENTY MILES LONG, HE USES THE LOO IN INVERNESS WHICH ACCOUNTS FOR THE TERRIBLE PONG!

Please remember NOT to spoil or damage any real walls by writing on them.

Answer page

Looking at handwriting

	Reshma	Weedy	Claudia	Mark	Emma	Roger	Lisa	You
Is it easy to read?	X	X	✓	✓	X	X	✓	
Are the letters on the line?	✓	X	X	✓	✓	✓	✓	
Are the capital letters in the right place?	✓	✓	✓	X	✓	✓	✓	
Are all the letters the right way round?	✓	X	✓	✓	X	✓	✓	
Are the letter tops high enough?	✓	✓	✓	✓	X	X	✓	
Are the letter tails long enough?	✓	✓	✓	✓	X	X	✓	
Are the spaces between the words right?	X	✓	✓	✓	X	✓	✓	

Don't be a Space Invader

This is how Sara's story looks when there are spaces between the words.

A Space Story

In fourteen hundred and ninety one the brave Sea Captain Christina Cucumber set out to sail across the Atlantic Ocean to prove that the world was round. She sailed on and on until one day she and her ship fell off the edge of the world. She had discovered that the world was round after all and she had also become the first Captain of a spaceship.

James Bong's capital letter

Miss Moneypincher's secret message is:

GET HATCHET AND GUS BEFORE THEY GET ME AAAAGH TOO LATE

Check your handwriting powers!

At last, your last page and Sid's not here! So write and border this page how you like.

You could copy out your favourite poem. You could write a short story or poem of your own. Try using these words (in any order):
slugs   handbag
jelly   gorilla

You could score it as you did on page 11.

Don't forget to keep your writing on the lines. Bye.

Remember your letter tops and tails. Bye.

Not too big, not too small. Bye.

Make sure it's easy to read. Bye.

No letters back to front. OR ELSE... Bye.

Don't forget to do it in your best joined up handwriting. And why not show your mum or dad, and get them to read page 24?

HOW THIS BOOK *works*

Sit down together to look at the book. Read the advice on pages 2 and 3 and then help your child start one of the activities just to get the feel of it. Look at the other pages too — there's lots of **FUN**.

Once started, **PRAISE** your child's first efforts, then just let them work independently. One of the great things about *SUCCESS!* is that you don't have to be there all the time. Do make sure, though, that you're around if your child needs your help or wants to show you what they've done.

HOW TO *CHECK* YOUR CHILD'S HANDWRITING POWERS

Try page 23 when most activities are finished. If your child wants to write a story or poem of their own, encourage them to draft it on rough paper first and then write it here in their best handwriting.

Help them to assess their own handwriting. If they're not sure how to do this, look together at the chart on page 11 and at the example of good handwriting on page 7. Praise what they've done — it will help **BUILD CONFIDENCE** if your child can identify the good points as well as the weak points in their handwriting.

HOW *you* CAN HELP

● If your child tends to print their letters and has problems with *joined up handwriting*, look again at the patterns suggested on page 5 and pages 8-9. The patterns are based on letter shapes: they're fun to do and are an excellent stepping stone from print script to joined up writing. ● Handwriting is a skill: to become proficient at any skill *practice* is essential. Encourage your child to practise whenever possible. Suggest and support handwriting activities: for example, sending letters or postcards to friends. ● Remember though that there is no one *style* of handwriting. Provided that your child's handwriting is legible and fluent, an individual style should be praised rather than suppressed. ● Provide a range of *writing tools* (e.g. pencils, ink pens, ball points, felt tips, etc.) and lots of paper. Scrap paper and different pens are a must for experimenting and scribbling. ● Don't expect too much. *Look for progress* and improvement rather than simply at the 'standard' of writing. Saving and dating examples of your child's handwriting can help you recognise that, although not yet fully proficient, your child's handwriting skills are improving.

You don't have to be an expert to make a *Success!*